More **LONDON MIDLAND STEAM** in the north-west

MORE
LONDON MIDLAND STEAM IN THE NORTH-WEST

N. F. W. DYCKHOFF

D. BRADFORD BARTON LIMITED

Frontispiece: The logical choice of locomotive most representative of developed L.M.S. steam practice would probably be the Stanier "Black Five"; No. 45313, from Springs Branch shed, accelerates a southbound express freight past Bamfurlong, between Wigan and Warrington, on 12 October 1964.

 © *copyright D. Bradford Barton Ltd 1975*   *ISBN 0 85153 219 5*

printed in Great Britain by H. E. Warne Ltd, London and St. Austell

for the publishers

D. BRADFORD BARTON LTD · **Trethellan House** · **Truro** · **Cornwall** · **England**

introduction

That I have been a railway enthusiast since child-hood is attributed by my family to our living the earliest years of my life in a house rented from the London Midland & Scottish Railway Company. Be that as it may, my first memories are of red engines hurtling under the footbridge at Didsbury station bringing me mingled joy and terror, and that special scent compounded of steam and coal smoke. It was hardly surprising then that as soon as I could lay hands on a camera I should set out to capture my enthusiasm in pictures.

My railway photographs in the North West cover two main periods; the early 1950's which began with my first publishable photographs and ended when I went up to university, and the mid-1960's when I came back to Manchester and saw out the last years of steam.

This volume is arranged in the form of a journey along the lineside and, with occasional detours, the route runs: Lancaster (Castle) to Crewe; ex-L.N.W.R.: Crewe to Manchester (London Road); ex-L.N.W.R.: Manchester (Victoria) to Wigan (Wallgate); ex-L. & Y.R.: Wigan (Central) to Manchester (Central); ex-G.C.R. and C.L.C.: Manchester (Central) to Stockport (Tiviot Dale); ex-C.L.C. and M.R.: Stock-port (Tiviot Dale) to Glazebrook; ex-C.L.C.

In choosing and captioning the photographs I have tried to show the classes of locomotive working in the area at the time, and also to dwell a little on locations and subjects, including such details as nicknames and liveries, not usually covered. A section is devoted to the Cheshire Lines Committee which, before Nationalisation, was one-third owned by the L.M.S. and which, after 1948, became part of London Midland Region. With very heavy goods traffic, particularly on the Manchester avoiding line, and often rural surroundings, the C.L.C. had a character entirely of its own.

Cameras used over the years have ranged from an Agfa Karat through Retina, Leica and Wrayflex to a vintage Super Ikonta which I have still. With its 6×9 cm negative size, this gives excellent results with modern emulsions. Photographs taken with all these cameras feature in this volume and con-sequently there is a variation in technical quality whatever the artistic merit or interest value of any particular picture.

Turning the pages, while giving the pleasure of happy days past, leaves an abiding sadness that something that was only a machine and yet had such beauty in itself that it could lighten even the industrial North, has passed away forever. As the last form of motive power whose power was visible and openly expressed, the steam locomotive had an attraction strong enough to survive its demise and to move its lovers to nostalgia at the slightest excuse. Romantic sentiments perhaps, but I hope that this book will provide not only just such an excuse for nostalgia, but will also be a consolation to those unlucky enough to have missed part of the Age of Steam.

On 17 May 1951, Class 2P 0-4-4
No. 41902, from Gloucester she
has its tanks filled at Lancaster
(Castle) station.   Half this clas
were transferred to Lancaster
shed to run the service to
Morecambe and Heysham via
Lancaster (Green Ayre) when
the 25 cycle AC 6,000 volt electr
trains of 1908 were withdrawn a
too expensive to maintain. Late
the system was converted to
50 cycle AC, and used for the
successful high voltage
experiments which led to the
adoption of new standards for
the present British Rail
electrification programme.

Stanier 'Princess Coronation'
Class 8P No. 46242 *City of
Glasgow* restarts a northbound
express from Lancaster (Castle)
station in May 1951. The
locomotive has the cut-away
smokebox front carried by those
engines which had their stream-
lined casing removed in the late
1940's. This feature disappeared
when the smokeboxes were
renewed between 1952 and 1960.

Ex-L. & Y. Class 2P 2-4-2T No. 50639 at Preston on station pilot duty. Although still in L.M.S. livery in May 1951, the locomotive has received its new British Railways number.

The 'Princess Coronation' class were the most powerful Pacifics ever to work in Great Britain and looked it. In the red livery—called maroon, but very close in colour to L.M.S. crimson lake—which sixteen of these locomotives received between December 1957 and November 1958, No. 46240 *City of Coventry* takes water at Wigan (North Western) while hauling a Carlisle-Crewe parcels train on 7 September 1964. This was one of the last duties for these locomotives prior to their withdrawal the same month. All the survivors except No. 46256 *Sir William A. Stanier, F.R.S.* were withdrawn from service on 12 September 1964.

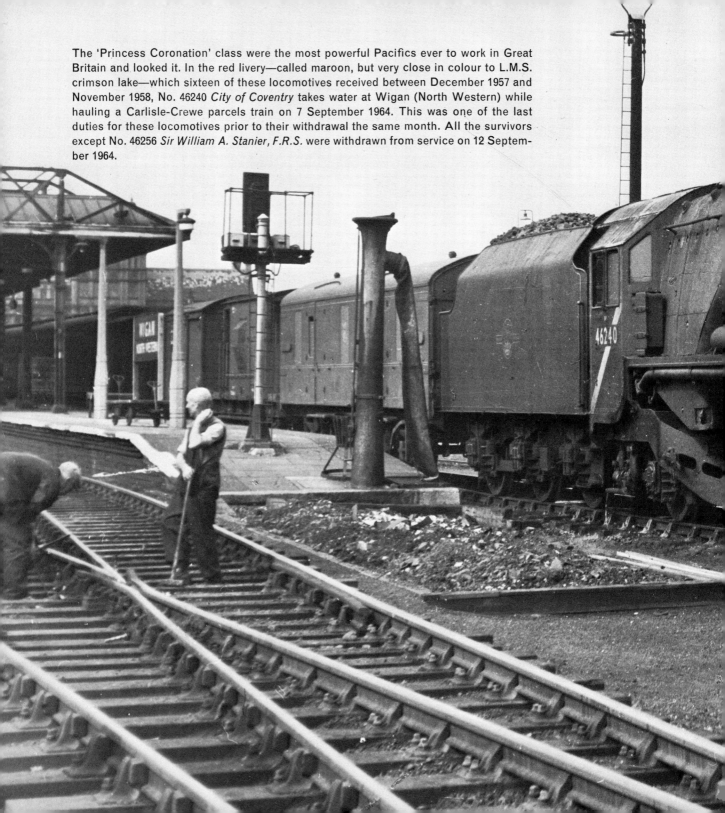

Class 5 4-6-0 No. 44818 brings the up 'Lakes Express', one of the last named expresses to be regularly steam-hauled on the West Coast main line, into Wigan (North Western) on 5 August 1964. Although British Railways adopted the policy in 1951 that all named trains should carry headboards, a few of the named trains on the London Midland Region, including 'The Lakes Express', were exempted because the locomotive working arrangements were too complicated.

Two months earlier, the same train leaving Wigan (North Western), on this occasion hauled by No. 45339.

The same afternoon Class 5 No. 45073 heads south out of Wigan with the up 'Lakes Express'. This train, which ran in the summer months, had through carriages from Workington (Main), Keswick, Windermere and Blackpool (North) and ran to London (Euston).

Class 8P 4-6-2 No. 46243 *City of Lancaster*, the last of the class to be de-streamlined in 1949, and seen here in B.R. maroon livery, speeds a Glasgow to Birmingham train past Windley Power Station on the outskirts of Wigan; 27 August 1964. Officially known as the 'Princess Coronation' class, these locomotives were variously known as the "Coronation" "Duchess" or "City" class after the different names carried by the individual locomotives.

13

On 10 March 1965 'Britannia' Class 7MT 4-6-2 No. 70054 *Dornoch Firth* speeds past Springs Branch with a Carlisle to Crewe train.

Framed by an L.M.S. signal gantry, Class 5 No. 45061 restarts a freight at Springs Branch on 2 November 1964. In the background, withdrawn locomotives wait outside the shed to be sent for scrap.

e L.M.S. Standard class of 0-6-0T was introduced in 1924 and popularly known as "Jinties"; No. 47395 ves Springs Branch to run light engine to Wigan station; 9 March 1965.

andard Class 4MT
. 75058, from
rings Branch shed,
banking duty at
mfurlong, 12
tober 1964. Built at
rindon in 1953, for
ndon Midland
gion, this engine
ginally had a 4,725
llon flush tender
milar to that fitted
Class 5MT No.
30 seen on page 26)
tead of the 5,000
llon tender with
ich it is seen here.

Class 5 No. 45005,
with an inspection
coach, receives clear
signals at Crompton
Sidings signal box
prior to joining the
main line. The upper
quadrant signal with
tubular post and
Nichol arms is an
L.M.S. standard
design, as is the
signal box.

More than 50 'lowflats' make up a special train as it rattles past Bamfurlong, hauled by Class 5 No. 45252, 12 October 1964.

On 29 May 1964, 'Britannia' No. 70039 *Sir Christopher Wren,* from Carlisle (Kingmoor) shed, passes the site of Bamfurlong station, closed in 1950, with an express freight heading south. The SC on the smokebox door denoted a self-cleaning smokebox.

'Britannia' No. 70042 *Lord Roberts*, steaming hard, heads a London to Blackpool train at Golborne, 26 March 1964. The bridge in the background carried the ex-G.C.R. branch from Lowton St. Mary's to St. Helens.

An up parcels train on 18 April 1964 approaching Golborne hauled by Class 5 No. 45371. The footbridge in the distance spanned all four tracks and was the view point from which the photograph above was taken.

A fitted goods runs south past Winwick with 'Britannia' No. 70021 *Morning Star* in charge; 11 March 1965. Below, rebuilt 'Royal Scot' Class 7P No. 46118 *Royal Welch Fusilier* brings an up parcels train along the straight stretch of track between Bamfurlong and Golborne; 23 March 1964.

Deputising for a failed diesel multiple unit on 28 August 1964, Ivatt Class 2 2-6-2T No. 41286 heads a push-and-pull unit at Bryn station forming the 6.15 p.m. Wigan (North Western) to Liverpool (Lime Street) local. Following its withdrawal from the St. Helens to Earlestown service, this combination was held in reserve at St. Helens for eventualities such as this.

The 11.00 a.m. SX Windermere-Crewe train passing Winwick Junction on 11 March 1965, with 'Britannia' No. 70012 *John of Gaunt* at its head. The tracks to the left join the Manchester-Liverpool route at Earlestown and were the original main line. The train is leaving the direct Golborne to Winwick Junction cut-off opened in 1864; in the distance can be seen the Vulcan Locomotive Works.

Designed at Derby and built at Crewe, the 'Britannia' class were the first British 2-cylinder Pacifics and when new were sent to Southern, Eastern, Western and Scottish Regions. In later years they returned to London Midland Region. One of the Western Region batch is seen at Winwick in March 1965—No. 70022 *Tornado* on a down mixed goods. Even without nameplates this can be recognised as an ex-Western Region 'Britannia' by its windshields. Following an accident in 1955, the handrails were removed from the windshields and hand holes substituted. The Western Region fitted six—other regions found two to be sufficient.

No. 45694 *Bellerophon* takes a down goods past Winwick on 11 March 1965. This locomotive was one of the 'Jubilee' class painted in British Railways experimental light green livery in 1948. Seen here in standard B.R. dark green, but without lining, it has the yellow prohibition stripe on the cab side identifying those locomotives banned south of Crewe after September 1964.

Fresh from the shops and in immaculate dark green livery, 'Patriot' Class 6P No. 45503 *The Royal Leicestershire Regiment* restarts a goods at the entrance to Hartford station north of Crewe. The first members of this class, introduced between 1930 and 1933, and nicknamed "Baby Scots", were nominally a Fowler rebuild of the Claughton class locomotives.

Another down freight at the same location hauled by a B.R. Standard Class 5MT. This class, designed at Doncaster and introduced in 1951, could be considered the final development of the Stanier 4-6-0, utilising this boiler in conjunction with wheels, valve gear and other detail from the 'Britannia' Pacifics. No. 73130 was built at Derby in 1956 for the Western Region and has Caprotti valve gear.

New from Crewe works on 28 April 1954, 'Britannia' 4-6-2 No. 70008 *Black Prince*, destined for Eastern Region, stands on one of the turntable roads at Crewe South, next to 'Black Five' No. 45129—the latter built sixteen years earlier by Armstrong Whitworth.

Inside Crewe South shed, ex-L.N.W.R. Webb Class 2F 0-6-2T No. 58888, one of the 'Coal Tanks' first introduced in 1882, stands newly renumbered and repainted in British Railways goods locomotive livery of unlined black.

The northbound 'Royal Scot' leaving Crewe in April 1951 hauled by 'Princess Coronation' Class No. 46221 *Queen Elizabeth.* The locomotive is in B.R. standard express passenger livery of blue with black and white lining, the coaches being in crimson lake and cream. The decorated engine headboard and the carriage roof boards with a backing of Stuart Royal tartan had been introduced the year before.

A close-up of No. 46221, taken a few minutes earlier, standing under the footbridge which ran from Crewe station to Crewe works—a favourite spotting post for railway enthusiasts.

Class 4P 2-6-4T No. 42363, of the Fowler parallel boiler design introduced in 1927, storms through Holmes Chapel station with a train from Crewe to Manchester (London Road). Because of the low platforms at this station steps up to the carriage doors were still available for use, and can be seen on the up platform.

No longer able to be called a 'Crimson Rambler', three-cylinder 'Compound' Class 4P 4-4-0 No. 41159, in mixed traffic livery of black with red, cream and grey lining and with British Railways in full on the tender, leaving Wilmslow with a train for Crewe on 21 April 1951.

A stopping train from Macclesfield (Central) to Manchester (London Road) runs into Adlington station hauled by Stanier Class 4P 2-6-4T No. 42567. This line branched from the L.N.W.R. Crewe-Manchester route at Cheadle Hulme, linking with the North Staffordshire Railway at Macclesfield.

At Cheadle Hulme in 1951 a Euston-Manchester (London Road) express, via Stoke, hauled by No. 46149 *The Middlesex Regiment,* runs in to join the line from Crewe. This locomotive, built in 1927 and rebuilt in 1945, originally carried the name *Lady of the Lake* and an etched brass plaque depicting the old time locomotive whose name it had been given.

On a running-in turn from Crewe to London Road, 'Royal Scot' No. 46148 *The Manchester Regiment* coasts into Alderley Edge station. She is newly rebuilt and in the B.R. dark green livery, with orange and black lining which became standard for all express passenger classes when blue was discontinued in 1951. No. 46148 was of the last 'Scot' rebuilds, being converted to the taper boiler version in July 1954.

With a bent running plate showing evidence of a collision, ex-L.M.S. 'Compound' No. 41168 pulls out of Stockport (Edgeley) station. Built at Vulcan Foundry in 1925, this was the last member of its class to be withdrawn by British Railways, in July 1961.

At the same platform a few minutes later, and also in September 1954, waits Class 3P 2-6-2T No. 40014. This parallel boilered class was designed by Fowler and represented a scaled down version of his 1927 design of 2-6-4T, but was not as successful. The small version of the first B.R. emblem is seen on the tank side—a larger version was used for express passenger classes.

A magnificent L.N.W.R. signal gantry dominates the skyline at Heaton Norris just north of Stockport. Passing underneath is a special train of L.N.E.R. stock hauled by 'Jubilee' No. 45724 *Warspite*. The coach behind the engine is one of the distinctive G.C.R. "Barnum" saloons designed for excursion traffic and built at Dukinfield Carriage & Wagon Works in 1910.

Some of the London Road to Crewe locals were regular turns for express passenger locomotives from Crewe North shed. 'Princess Royal' Class 8P No. 46211 *Queen Maud*, in British Railways mixed traffic livery, heads a rake of suburban coaches newly painted in the all-over crimson lake livery used for non-gangway coaching stock, past Heaton Norris No. 3 Box in the autumn of 1954.

7F 0-8-0 No. 49428, one of the ex-L.N.W.R. Bowen-Cooke simple two-cylinder superheated G2 class built 1921-22, trundles the Gorton breakdown train in the direction of Manchester between Heaton Norris and Heaton Chapel.

A stopping freight train hauled by Class 5 No. 45256 passing Heaton Mersey station, newly rebuilt in connection with the electrification of the line from Manchester (Piccadilly) to Crewe, in September 1964.

The line to Sheffield (Victoria) from Manchester (Piccadilly)—formerly called Manchester (London Road)—was electrified throughout in the early 1950's. Class 4F 0-6-0 No. 44160, shunts under the wires at Guide Bridge on 18 September 1964.

Three views at Heaton Chapel and Heaton Moor station in the early 1950's. An ex-M.R. 0-6-0 hustles its goods train along the down slow line (left) whilst opposite No. 44715 emerges from under the gantry on the slow line, with an up express. The spectacle glasses have been removed from the sighting arms of the L.N.W.R. signals, probably to save the lamp man a sixty foot climb. Below, Class 4P 2-6-4T No. 42578 runs through the station on the fast line with a Manchester to Buxton train. Situated between the up and down fast lines, the diminutive signal box had only twelve levers, and was demolished in 1954.

Class 5 No. 44819 starting a Blackpool train out of Manchester (Victoria) station, 9 November 1963. The mixed traffic livery is clearly visible, together with the more heraldically correct emblem introduced in 1957 to replace the previous 'lion astride a wheel'.

e changing order at Manchester (Victoria) station in September 1964. Class 5 No. 45072
its with a Barrow train while Type 4 English Electric No. D291 has just arrived with a
in from Windermere and a diesel multiple unit stands at the far platform.

On 'Wall-Side Pilot' duty at Manchester (Victoria), ex-L.M.S. Class 2 2-6-0 No. 46418 poses for its photograph. Known by spotters as "Mickey Mice", these were an Ivatt design introduced in 1946 and building was continued by British Railways; 9 November 1963.

The second 'Wall-side Pilot' on duty on 9 November 1963 was ex-M.R. Class 4F 0-6-0 No. 43952. In the interval before its next duty, the fireman pushes coal forward on the tender.

No. 73141, one of the Standard Class 5MT locomotives fitted with Caprotti valve gear, brings the coaches which are to form the 10.50 a.m. train to Wigan (North Western) into Manchester (Exchange); 18 September 1964.

Back on one of its old regular routes for a farewell appearance, Hughes Class 5P ex-L. & Y. 4-6-0 No. 50455, the last survivor of the "Dreadnoughts", heading a half day excursion from Blackpool and other north-west towns to the Railway Museum at York on 1 July 1951. This locomotive was one of a batch of twenty built by the L.M.S. in 1924 using parts originally intended for further 4-6-4T engines—at the last moment it was decided that tender engines would be more useful.

Class 5 2-6-0 No. 42712, one of the Hughes-designed locomotives built in 1926 under Fowler's direction and fitted with a standard Midland tender noticeably narrower than the cab, pulls off the main line at Agecroft Junction with a train of empty coal wagons, January 1966. As is now well-known, because of the ungainly appearance caused by their running plates being set high to provide clearance for the large outside cylinders, these locomotives were nicknamed 'Crabs'.

Early on a January morning in 1966 'Britannia' No. 70017 *Arrow* passes Agecroft colliery
and power station with an express for Manchester.

2-6-4T No. 42601, of the Stanier Class 4P taper boiler design introduced in 1935, coasting into Atherton (Central) station with the 5.28 p.m. Manchester (Victoria) to Wigan (Wallgate) on 1 July 1964.

Daisy Hill station has a name worthy of a Betjeman poem. Seen here on 3 July 1964 is 2-6-4T No. 42435 with the 6.05 p.m. Manchester (Victoria) to Southport local.

A Bolton (Trinity Street) to Liverpool (Exchange) train enters Wigan (Wallgate) hauled by Class 5 No. 44809, July 1964.

A mixed freight emerging from Wigan (Wallgate) station headed by Class 5 2-6-0 No. 42952. These moguls were one of the first standard designs produced by Stanier for the L.M.S. when he became C.M.E. Only forty were built but they were found all over the system on a variety of duties.

A few days earlier, on 29 June, the same locomotive on the climb out of Wigan (Wallgate) past the North Western station with the 12.40 p.m. Liverpool (Exchange) to Rochdale train.

The third station in Wigan—Central—was absorbed by the Great Central Railway in 1906, together with the branch to the C.L.C. Manchester-Liverpool line at Glazebrook West Junction. Opened in 1892, it was closed in November 1964. On 27 August 1964 Stanier 2-6-4T No. 42465 waits to leave with the 1.00 p.m. train for Manchester (Central). Although much of the station has already been demolished, enough remains to show the building's distinctive style. The G.C.R. signalling has gone, but their parachute water column remains.

Later that afternoon No. 42465 returns with the 5.09 p.m. Partington to Wigan (Central), seen here drawing to a halt at Lower Ince station. In the background condemned carriages are waiting to be cut up on the sidings of the Central Wagon Coy., Wigan.

Hindley South signal box with the 5.25 p.m. SX Irlam to Wigan (Central) train hauled by Class 4P No. 42634, leaving Hindley station. The elaborate sighting arrangements on the signal box are a point of interest; 27 August 1964.

The 12.07 p.m. S.O. Manchester (Central) to Warrington (Central) train coasts past Padgate signal box—no longer in use by this date in September 1964—with Stanier 2-6-4T No. 42644 in charge.

Lowton St. Mary station was opened in April 1884 and like the other stations on the line changed very little with the passing years. On 22 April 1964. Fairburn Class 4P 2-6-4T No. 42076 brings the 5.33 p.m. train from Manchester (Central), terminating at Lowton St. Mary, in to the platform.

Shadows fall across Class 5 No. 44815 as it heads a local train for Manchester (Central) between Urmston and Trafford Park in March 1966.

In August 1964 a Manchester (Central) to Liverpool (Central) train enters Glazebrook station hauled by 2-6-4T No. 42076. This locomotive was one of 277 built from 1945 onwards as the Fairburn development of Stanier's design, with a shorter wheelbase and detail alterations. The station, an important one on the C.L.C., was a splendid example of Victorian railway architecture, even to the employee cottages on the down platform.

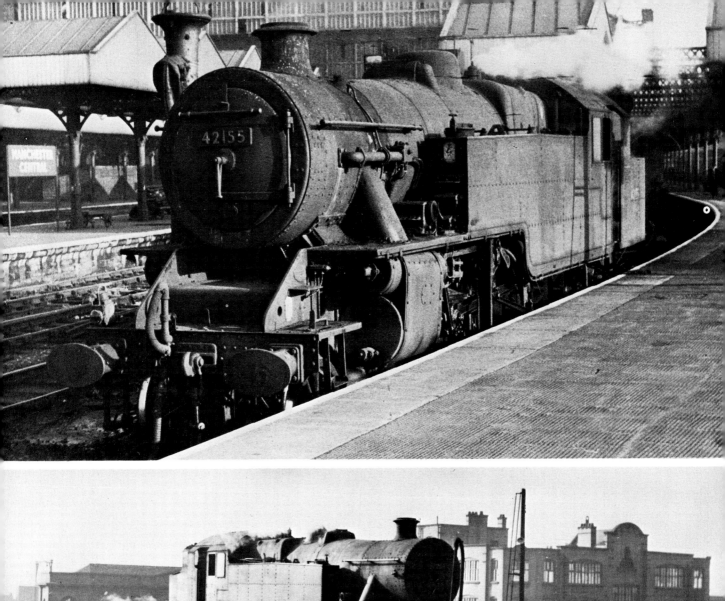

Scenes at Manchester Central). This station was opened to the public in July 1880 and its segmentally shaped roof with a span of 210 ft is only exceeded by St. Pancras (240 ft.). Closed in May 1969, it became a temporary car park while a decision was made on its future. One of the Fairburn 2-6-4Ts, No. 42155, waits at the platform end on February 1964. Although with increased standardisation nicknames became less common, these locomotives were known as 'Teddy Bears'.

On the same day another locomotive of this class, No. 42064, being turned on the manually operated turntable. On 18 April 1964, Class 5 No. 45466 leaves with empty stock.

Declining patronage has reduced the SO 12.10 p.m. train from Manchester (Central) to Cheadle Heath, Stockport, to two coaches, as it pulls away from Chorlton Junction on 26 September 1964 hauled by Fairburn 2-6-4T No. 42134.

Ten years later the Midland route to London had been closed, the track lifted and vandals have taken over. The scene contrasts sadly with that on the opposite page, for not only has steam departed but so have many of the railways of the North West.

Views at Withington and West Didsbury station in 1954.   Above, a Manchester (Central)-St. Pancras express heading south with 'Jubilee' Class 6P 4-6-0 No. 45579 *Punjab*, immaculate in dark green livery. Possibly because of their Great Western ancestry these locomotives wore this colour particularly well. In 1957 *Punjab* attained the highest authenticated speed for its class of $97\frac{1}{2}$ m.p.h. Opposite, a local train waits to leave for Manchester (Central) hauled by Stanier Class 3P 2-6-2T No. 40089. Some of the Midland station awnings on the up platform have been removed—early evidence of the lessening importance of this line.

An empty wagon train rattles past the down platform headed by Class 4F 0-6-0 No. 43870, one of the Fowler superheated design introduced by the Midland in 1911.

On a snowy morning in January 1952, Class 3P 2-6-2T No. 40094 steams away from Withington past the Didsbury distant at caution. These locomotives were Stanier's 1935 taper boiler development of the Fowler version. Although a relative failure, 139 were built between 1935-38.

Standard Class 5MT
No. 73014 starts a
Manchester (Central)
to Derby slow train
out of Withington
and West Didsbury
station.

'Jubilees' were the
mainstay of the
express trains on the
Midland line to London
for many years—often
with deplorable effects
on timekeeping. A
typical young train
spotter watches No.
45655 *Keith*
approaching
Didsbury station. The
Midland down starting
signal with sight
boards was a notable
survival, not being
replaced by a
colour light signal
until 1956.

In June 1951 and retaining the L.M.S. postwar express passenger locomotive livery of glossy black with maroon and straw lining and insignia sanserif style, but with B.R. number, 'Jubilee' No. 45696 *Arethusa* leaves Heaton Mersey with a Derby to Manchester (Central) stopping train. Some of the coaches are also still in L.M.S. livery, while others have been repainted in the B.R. livery for gangwayed stock of crimson lake and cream with black and gold lining.

A freight, having stopped by the signal box, restarts away from Heaton Mersey hauled by Class 4 2-6-0 No. 43120. This design by Ivatt was introduced in 1947 and building was continued by British Railways until a total of 162 had been constructed.

A sunny spring morning in 1952 as 'Jubilee' No. 45602 *British Honduras* heads under the footbridge at Didsbury. At this station the awnings, still complete although the glazing has been removed, show the scale of commuter traffic once catered for by the 'South District' line.

Class 5 No. 44986 makes a determined recovery from a signal check at Didsbury station and pulls out past the goods yard with the 11.35 a.m. Manchester-Derby, with through carriages to Nottingham. No. 44986 was paired with this self-weighing tender for many years —here, in 1951, the tender is still in L.M.S. livery.

Together with Withington and West Didsbury, Heaton Mersey station was closed in July 1961 although Didsbury remained open until 1967. Early in 1964, Standard Class 4MT No. 75057 steams by with a trip goods. The station footbridge as well as linking the platforms carried a public footpath over the railway. This class of locomotive, though built at Brighton, was developed from the L.M.S. 2-6-4T to provide a larger working range.

Under a snow-laden sky a Class 4F 0-6-0 shunts Heaton Mersey goods yard in the winter of 1951-52. The signalman takes the opportunity to stock up with coal for his stove.

Springtime in Cheshire, with Class 8F 2-8-0 No. 48683, one of the locomotives built by the Southern Railway during the Second World War, disturbing the rural peace near Cheadle with an I.C.I. limestone train from Derbyshire.

Stockport (Tiviot Dale) station closed in January 1967 when it lost its service to Manchester (Central). The service, via the C.L.C. route, to Warrington and Liverpool had ceased before then. Stanier Class 5 No. 44827 stands at the head of an all-stations train to Liverpool on 21 March 1964.

A Saturday holiday special to North Wales bursts from under the road bridge at Cheadle station hauled by 'Jubilee' 4-6-0 No. 45684 *Jutland*; 15 August 1964.

In 1967, with smoke number plate remov and cabside numbe invisible under the grime, a 'Space Shi B.R. Standard Clas 9F 2-10-0—heads an empty wagon train between Northende Junction and Chea

The light snow is beginning to thaw as a pair of Class 3F 0-6-0's roar through Cheadle station with a freight. The leading engine is No. 43191 from Derby shed— and the train engine is No. 43548; 26 January 1952.

The stalwarts of much L.M.S. freight work were the Fowler designed Standard Class 4 0-6-0 locomotives; No. 44501 at Northenden Junction with a mixed goods in the winter of 1963. The speed restriction sign on the right was designed by the L.N.E.R. and adopted for use by British Railways in 1956. The tall signals with lower quadrant arms on latticed posts were a feature of the line and survived the end of steam.

Hughes/Fowler 2-6-0's became common on this line in the mid 1960's. No. 42777, one of the batch built at Crewe in 1927, crosses the junction at Northenden with a mixed goods in April 1964.

Another regular performer was the Riddles-designed 'Austerity' Class WD 2-8-0. No. 90245 near Northenden station on 8 November 1963.

No. 49510, of the Fowler Class 7F 0-8-0's christened "Austin 7's" after their introduction in 1929, passes Northenden Junction signal box with a train of empty wagons in June 1951.

"Super D's"—ex-L.N.W.R. G1, G2a and G2 0-8-0 locomotives, together with their ex-L.M.S. counterpa shared much of the ex-C.L.C. mineral workings in the 1950's; No. 49451 brings a coal train round the cu between Cheadle and Northenden.

Class 8F No. 48275 makes an impressive sight as it speeds a mineral train towards Northenden Juncti January 1951.

On 4 July 1964 sister Class 4 No. 43046 enters Northenden station with the 11.40 a.m. Stockport (Tiviot Dale) to Warrington (Central). Note the tall signal box, raised to enable the signalman to see over the road bridge, and the signal for the junction—straight ahead for Cheadle C.L.C. and right for Cheadle L.N.W.R. (closed 1917)—in the distance.

Not the most successful of engines when first introduced—when they had a double chimney—the Ivatt Class 4 2-6-0's were not the most beautiful of engines and acquired the nickname "Doodlebugs", or later, "Clodhoppers". The driver of No. 43048 at the head of a platelayers' special leaving Northenden Junction catches sight of the photographer and opens the regulator sharply.

With additional brake vans at the front, another empty wagon train is headed by Stanier Class 5 No. 45039 running tender first, between Baguley and Northenden; 27 November 1965.

Class 8F No. 48156 on a coal train passing Northenden station; 10 October 1964.

As steam was displaced from the main lines, express passenger locomotives appeared on a variety of more humble duties. 'Jubilee' No. 45612 *Jamaica* approaching Baguley with a train of oil tanks from Cheadle Junction for Ellesmere Port. The date is 8 February 1964, and No. 45612 is in the unlined green livery which, for reasons of economy, was used when the time for withdrawal from service approached. Also, to avoid theft, the nameplates have been removed.

Austerity 2-8-0 No. 90157 thunders through Baguley station with a train of empty wagons from Partington Junction, February 1964. This was one of the busiest sections of the ex-C.L.C. with trains often queuing at Skelton Junction before running on to clear Northenden Junction.

Overleaf: Class 5 4-6-0 No. 45103 puts on a special display for the camera and whistles for a sound recorder as it blasts past Baguley signal box with a Godley-Northwich freight, 8 February 1964.

On 8 February 1964 a Godley to Partington Junction coal train passes Baguley station hauled by Class 8F No. 48403, one of the locomotives built by the G.W.R. between 1943 and 1945. As well as those built by the S.R. and G.W.R., locomotives of this class were also built by the L.N.E.R. for their own use, and by the North British Locomotive Company for the War Department. All eventually came to London Midland Region to make the total more than 660.

A solitary ganger continues to work on the up line as Class 8F No. 48212 approaches with an empty wagon train; Baguley, 31 March 1965.

Ex-Crosti boilered Standard Class 9F No. 92022, rebuilt with conventional exhaust arrangements, running light towards Northenden. Photographed outside Baguley from one of the Stockport (Tiviot Dale) to Warrington (Central) local trains in March 1964.

Fairburn 2-6-4T No. 42113 leaves Baguley with the 5.20 p.m. SO Stockport (Tiviot Dale)-Liverpool train, 20 June 1964. Note the station porter's house on the left.

In wind and rain on
18 February 1964,
Standard Class 9F
No. 92159 approaching
West Timperley
station.

No. 42817 *Crab*
running through
Skelton East
Junction, from Skelto
West Junction where
the ex-C.L.C. lines
diverge—left to
Broadheath, Lymm an
Warrington and right
to West Timperley,
Glazebrook and
Liverpool. The track
branching to the right
in the photograph
curves round to join
the M.S.J.A. line and
then forms part of the
C.L.C. route to
Northwich.

With safety valves blowing off, Ivatt Class 4 2-6-0 No. 43033 enters Partington with an afternoon Stockport (Tiviot Dale) to Liverpool local. After leaving the station, the train climbs to cross the bridge over the Manchester Ship Canal which was opened in 1894— 21 years after the line from Skelton Junction to Glazebrook, and for which extensive new works were therefore required.

The guard gives the right away to the 4.56 p.m. Liverpool (Central) to Stockport (Tiviot Dale) train at Glazebrook station, 28 August 1964.